# The Great Big Book Of Memes

## *The Definitieve*
## *Book Of Funny Memes*

# Introduction

Thank you for purchasing this book: The Great Big Book Of Memes.

This book covers the topic of memes, and will teach you about what a meme is, what makes a meme, common memes as well as hundreds of memes for all to enjoy.

At the completion of this book your sides will be hurting from so much laughter and you should have a good understanding of what a meme is.

Once again, thanks for downloading this book, I hope you find it to be helpful!

# What Is A Meme?

If you have ever used the internet? Then you would have heard of memes but what are they?

A meme in most cases is a picture on the internet with a funny or relatable caption. They are created by people and then uploaded to the internet. Memes are then copied and spread quickly through the internet by users sharing them with their friends, family and even strangers through social media. Memes are not only pictures with captions but also can be videos and pieces of text such as text message conversations, twitter posts, Facebook posts and quotes from movies or famous people.

Memes are most commonly spread through social media. Facebook having hundreds, maybe thousands of pages dedicated to creating and sharing memes to the world.

The most common memes are quotes from movies or pictures from a movie with a caption. The caption may not be accurate to the movie, they will often vary or merge multiple movies or quotes together which is what makes them humorous.

Below is an example. The man is Mr Spock who is from Star Trek, the quote is "May the force be with you" which is from Star Wars and Dr Who isn't from either of those Sci Fi series but from his own tv show called Dr Who.

# Common Types of Memes

There are many types of memes. They can involve dogs, cats, sports stars, movie stars, cartoons, games and many more.

Some of the common memes found are listed below,

1. Crazy Girlfriend

This meme is simply a picture of a girl but she looks like she is crazy and obsessive. This meme generally will her being really controlling or protective towards her boyfriend or partner.

2. Stoned Guy

This one is a man who looks like he is very under the influence and doesn't know what's going on. These memes are generally him saying something so incredibly wrong or really stupid.

3. Grumpy Cat

This meme is a picture of a cat that just looks incredibly angry or grumpy. The cat always has some negative way to look at something no matter how happy or cheerful it may be.

## 4. Boromir "One Does Not Simply"

This meme is was created form a quote from the movie The Lord Of The Rings The Fellowship Of The Ring. The original quote was "One does not simply walk into Mordor." Theses memes generally just have a difficult task added onto the end of "One does not simply".

5. Kid Eating Sand

This meme is a picture of a boy at the beach eating some sand but the facial expression he makes with a fist full of sand makes it look like he is fist pumping. This meme is used for when you have a win or some good luck.

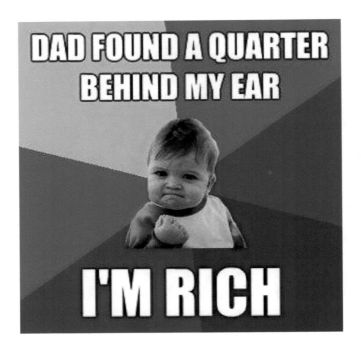

These are only a few of the common and more popular memes. New ones are made everyday. There are thousands of memes all different to each other.

Some people have become unexpectedly semi famous for being turned into a meme. Their fame will usually die just as quick as it grew. There are memes tailored for all different kinds of humor. You never know what could turn out to be the next big hit.

**By now you should have a good idea of what a meme is and what makes a meme.**

**Now without further adieu, here are the memes...**

when you wake up in the middle of the night to check your phone and it's on full brightness

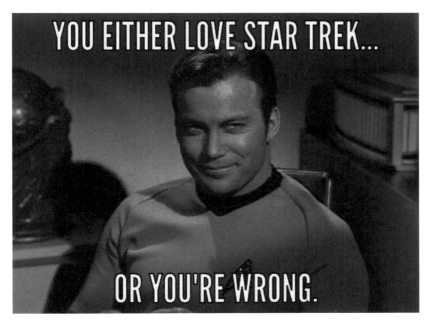

Why don't you like sand?

A: It's coarse
B: It's rough
C: It's irritating
D: It gets everywhere

MERRY CHRISTMAS

YA FILTHY ANIMAL

When you take your food out of the microwave and it burns your hand

WAITS WHOLE LIFE FOR ZOMBIE APOCALYPSE

GETS INFECTED IN HIS SLEEP

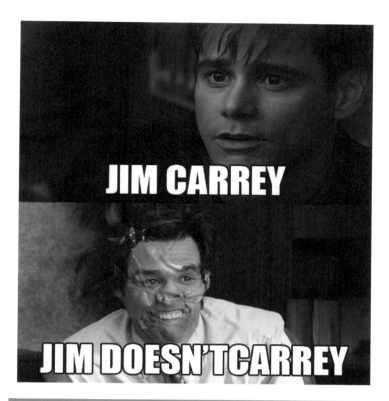

JIM CARREY

JIM DOESN'TCARREY

WHO NEEDS EXPERIENCE

WHEN YOU GOT SWAG

When the teacher is
watching you during
a test..

and you pretend
that you're at least
trying to think

PALEO BROWNIES, PALEO CUPCAKES, PALEO MUFFINS, PALEO COOKIES, PALEO FUDGE, PALEO BREAD...

PLEASE, TELL ME MORE ABOUT YOUR "HUNTER GATHERER" DIET...

when you eating an oreo and
dunk it in milk but it breaks off and
sinks to the bottom.

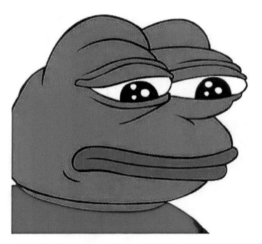

When you solve a maths
problem 3 times

and get different answer
each time

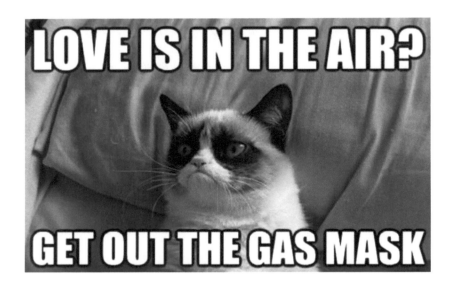

I'M ON A SEAFOOD DIET

I SEE FOOD AND I EAT IT.

PUT THE TREATS IN THE BOWL

AND NOBODY GETS HURT

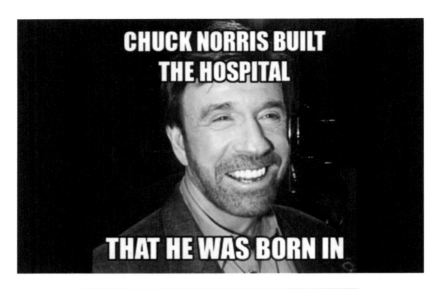

CHUCK NORRIS BUILT
THE HOSPITAL

THAT HE WAS BORN IN

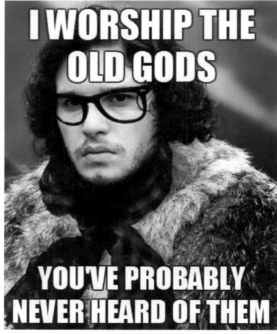

I WORSHIP THE
OLD GODS

YOU'VE PROBABLY
NEVER HEARD OF THEM

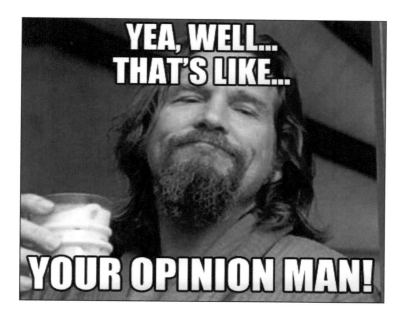

When people ask when I want to eat

Robber: Give me all you got on you.
Drake: Here...take my wallet....she already stole my heart....

When someone is about to remind
the teacher about the homework

After you tell somebody "bless
you" twice and they keep
sneezing

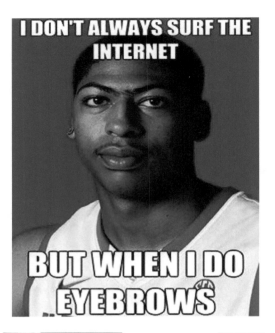

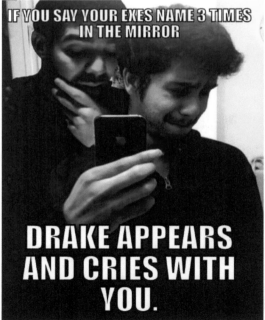

When he's testing the fuck outta you and your crazy bitch side bout to shine bright like a diamond

WHAT IF... ONE DAY GOOGLE WAS DELETED

AND WE COULDN'T GOOGLE WHAT HAPPENED TO GOOGLE

Roses are red,
Harambe's in heaven...

0:22    2:16

Unquestionable proof that Bush did 9/11

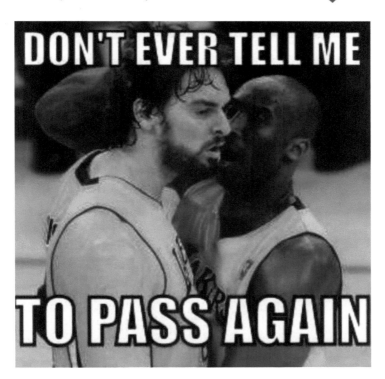

BEST MATHEMATICIANS 👀👀

HAHAHA
GREAT POST!

WELL MEME'D
MY FRIEND!

When I go back and read that text I sent him of me spazzing the fuck out and say to myself "I'm crazy" lmao

MOM SAYS: ALCOHOL IS YOUR ENEMY.

JESUS SAYS: LOVE YOUR ENEMY. CASE CLOSED.

What people think Boromir looks like when he says

"One does not simply"

What he really looks like.

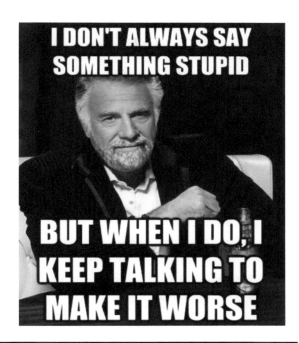

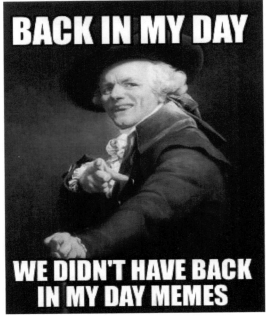

I BELIEVE THIS CAT IS

INBRED

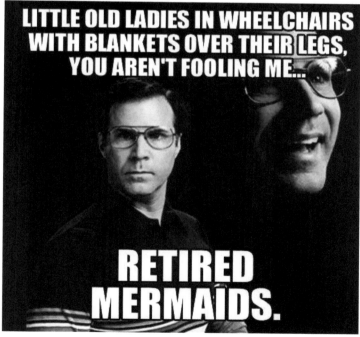

LITTLE OLD LADIES IN WHEELCHAIRS WITH BLANKETS OVER THEIR LEGS, YOU AREN'T FOOLING ME...

RETIRED MERMAIDS.

How do people starve like just eat
something bruh lol

When u promised to work out, do
laundry, clean and go to bed early, but
then get home from work and sit
there like this for 4 hours

When you see your bed after a
long day

Mom: You keep failing all your tests.
Son: Mom, the only test you ever passed was your pregnancy test.

Choose your fighter

When your nose is stuffed and you just sit there and think about the time when it wasn't stuffed and how you took breathing freely for granted

**Friend: shes so hot**

**Me: shes 14**

**Friend: age is just a number**

**Me: you know what else is just a number?**

**Friend: what?**

**Me:**

Lady: who is the worlds cutest lamp?

Cat: who is the worlds loneliest alcoholic?

Lady: wow

Cat: yeah fucking hurts doesn't it?

SCIENTIST: Let's name this spider Long Legs, for its long legs

SCIENTIST 2: Hmm not kinky enough

When the teacher randomly calls on you when you're spacing out

The answer is obtuse

If you get with me you will be $(Mg,Fe)_7Si_8O_{22}(OH)_2$

Cummingtonite

| General | |
|---|---|
| Category | Inosilicate |
| Chemical formula | $(Mg,Fe)_7Si_8O_{22}(OH)_2$ |
| Strunz classification | 09.DE.05 |
| Crystal symmetry | Monoclinic 2/m |
| Unit cell | a = 9.53 Å, b = 18.23 Å, c = 5.32 Å; β = 101.97°; Z = 2 |

just do it ✓

Did you just use a
saxophone as a Nike icon

Improvise. Adapt. Overcome

when you're chill but people
at the party are hyper af and
start screaming at you

When you check your phone in
the middle of the night, but forget
to turn the brightness down

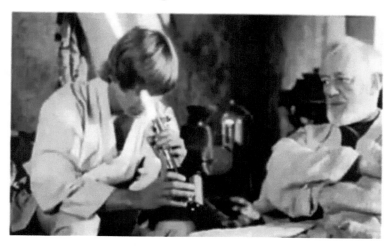

when your friend forgets to give you a
blanket

They always ask "who's a good boy"
never "hows the good boy"

do u ever just like flex your foot
wrong and it cramps and you're just
like

this is it

this is how it ends

Who ordered the shredded cheese?

# Who Would Win

### The Strongest Bone in The Body

### One Silver Boi

when you trying to watch netflix and she
pulls a titty out

# When you watch rick and morty

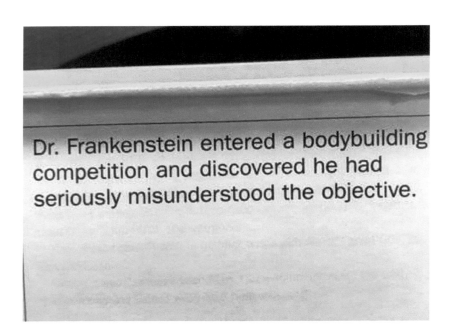

Dr. Frankenstein entered a bodybuilding competition and discovered he had seriously misunderstood the objective.

When someone opens the door to my room

you heard of Panic! At The Disco,
now get ready for

**You must be at least 6'2", workout, have a nice car, have strong shoulders, have a career, and a beard.**

**HER:**

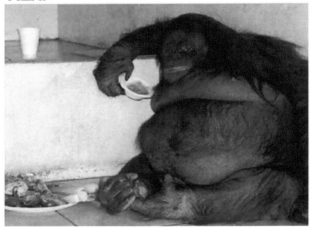

Friend: Do you want the rest of my-
Me:

when you try to eat a light dinner because you need to save room for all the ass you're going to eat later

When you watching Chopped and a chef decides to make a vinaigrette with less than a minute left

When the wknd is over and u have
to say goodbye to your real self for
a few days

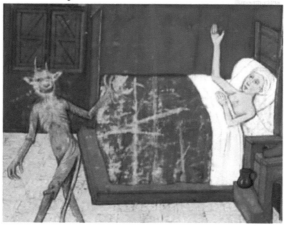

How I sleep knowing that I have a big day tomorrow and need as much rest as possible

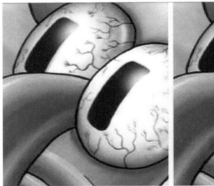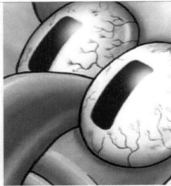

What's the time, Einstein?

Job Interviewer: so how flexible can your hours be?

Me:

When your teacher is telling her boring ass life story,but you need her to round your 58 to a 85

She was born to be an author

PAGE TURNER
BOOKS HAVE SOLD OVER A MILLION COPIES WORLDWIDE

# Who would win?

**Massively popular English language honed and perfected 1400 years**

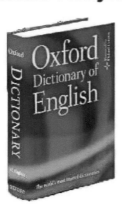

**Some guy that doesn't feel hot whilst wearing a jacket**

I hate when people just leave shopping carts in the middle of the aisle

*at a job interview*
Boss: What's ur biggest accomplishment?
Me:

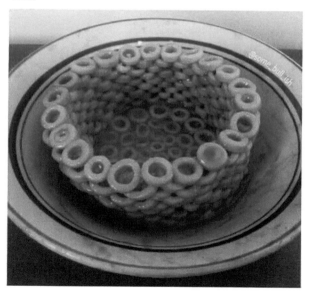

**CAN WE TAKE A SECOND TO APPRECIATE HOW MUCH THIS CHAIR LOOKS LIKE DUSTIN FROM STRANGER THINGS**

boy: why is the food cold and bland?

dad: because your mother put her heart and soul into it

**Remember this kid from stranger things? This is him now. Feel old yet?**

When you have to hold down the power button to turn off a device

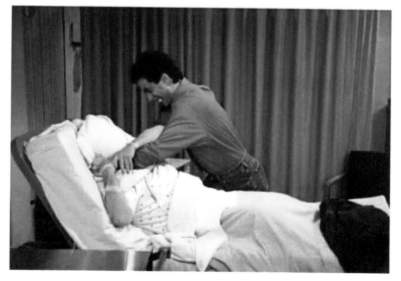

No lighter but we got science

i wanna get WASTED

W ake up early
A nticipate a productive day
S tay hydrated
T ake a multivitamin
E xercise
D ont stay up too late

10:20 AM - 23 Jul 2017

when you are sitting on your flight playing
csgo and your headphones disconnect as the
game loudly announces "Bomb has been planted"

## when someone asks why im single

mans not hot

Pro tip: If you're tired of boiling water when you make pasta, just boil a few gallons at the beginning of the week and freeze it for later.

**Hey kid wanna** study at Harvard **with us**

**No thanks I already** watch Rick and Morty

A very rare photograph of Michael
Jackson performing without his glove

When your cat knows you're vegan.

UPDATE. EA announces plans for next gen controller.

*Confused screaming*

When someone comes over
unannounced and catches you playing
all 4 players in a game of monopoly

'What do we call this'
Now Elon, this is what we call walking.
'And humans enjoy this?'
Yes Elon. Yes they do.

"Listen dude, sarcasm will get you nowhere in life"

"Well it got me to the Sarcasm World Championships in Peru back in 98"

"Really?"

"No"

Me: what's a good show to watch on netfli...
Person 3.2 miles away: HAVE YOU SEEN STRANGER THINGS

The only thing stranger than Stranger
Things is @SeanAstin 's 2005 wardrobe

 **Sean Astin** ✔ @SeanAstin · 1d
It's called fashion sweetie look it up

💬 270     🔁 571     ♡ 6,270

me carrying all this love but no one to
give it to

When I see a teacher make this face taking attendance, I know its my name.

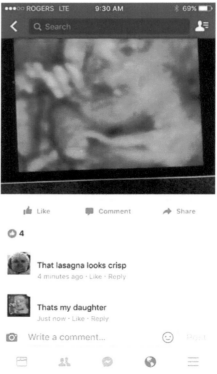

70% of single girls

Me: *Pours heart and soul into a text*
Her:

he is always watching

Me: Help, this man is dying. Does anyone know what I can do?

Stranger things fan: you should start watching, it's a reaaallyy good show

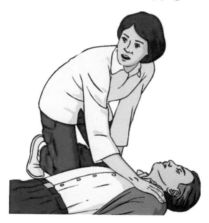

Found a brand new way to get your snacks into a movie

Finally we're being taught something that we can all relate to!

When your WiFi is down for ten minutes

Cop: ur car smells like marijuana

Me: whoever smelt it dealt it

Cop: gosh dangit

Me: ur under arrest

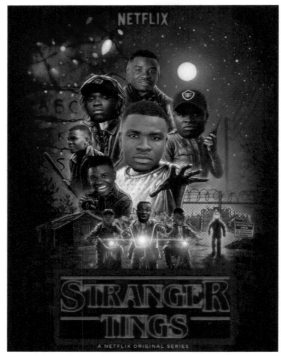

When your friends invite you to go out with them, you know you ain't going, but you act interested anyway

1-10: how much do you hate me?

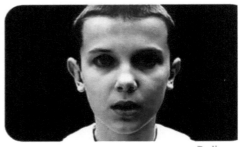

Delivere

Ok

Got it

After a year of telling my friend he looks like Bob Ross, he finally sends me this photo

When you spend most of your time looking at memes instead of getting shit done

when he brings you food>>>

My anxiety watching me try to make
small talk with someone I just met

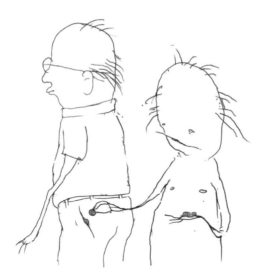

sneak a few blueberries into
a stranger's pocket so they
can have a little snack later.

When youtube gives you an
unskippable ad

Ultra rare picture of a vegan being born

# WHO WOULD WIN?

A whole institution designed to teach and train young humans in various fields

Cuddly boi

Flipper is the latest Hollywood celebrity accused of sexual assault

When u on AUX duty and u checking to see if the crew feeling it

People: are you ok?

Me: yea

Me to me: don't study that topic it
won't come up in the exam
*Reads first question*

When you leave ur dog at ur grandma's
house for a few days

When you are at Ikea and pronounce something right

Approaching the end of this semester like

that mini heart attack when you can't feel these in your pocket

When you invite a girl over to watch star wars, and she starts taking her clothes off

I don't think so

Bond: My watch says u r not a VIRGIN.

Girl: But I'm still a VIRGIN.

Bond: My watch is 20 mins fast.

Your girlfriend got pregnant, you never slept with her. She says She's a virgin. When the baby is born, three guys come out of nowhere with presents. What are you doing?

When you find pineapple in your pizza

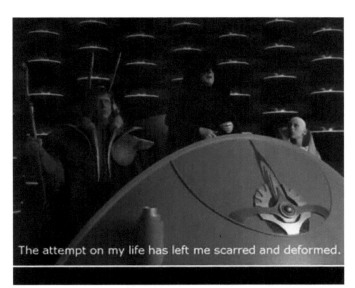

The attempt on my life has left me scarred and deformed.

when ur telling ur grandparents about ur job and they have no clue what ur talking bout but they're supportive

Use This Trick To Make Teacher Think You Are Studying While You're Eating Spaghetti

Me: Are you a wolf or a corgi?
Him: I don't know
Me: Send a pic

# Hipsters or Civil War soldiers?

Recipe wanted me to beat an egg. Y'all already know what's about to go down.

When your friend keeps handing you shots

"If you are good at something never do it for free"

Me:

Increasing the temperature bit by bit
during your shower to see how much
your body can take

me trying to fix my rapidly deteriorating
mental heath

# how to deal with a break up

**normal people:** cry, eat ice cream, watch sad movies, cry some more

**steve harrington:** adopt four middle-school kids and become the best single mom the hawkins high school basketball team has ever seen

throwback to last year when i made a snowman and it started to melt but refroze overnight

**BARACK OBAMA**
MICHELLE OBAMA'S HUSBAND

ah okay, that guy

When the cashier ignores your hand
and places your change on the table

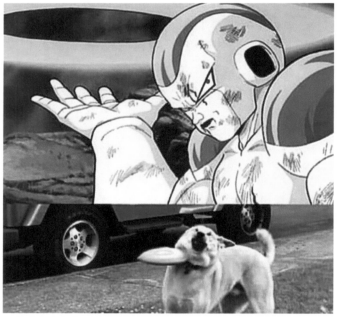

Guess who's looking at memes
instead of working

When you are high af and you have no idea how you got into a forest but it's kinda cool so you just accept it

YOU MATCHED WITH MIMI ON 9/16/17

 if you were a vegetable, you'd be a cutecumber 😉

If I was a vegetable I'd ask you to pull the plug and end my misery

Sent

Today 8:11 PM

 omg

# Remember Eleven & Mike?
## Here they are now. Feel old yet?

Just found a penguin skeleton in the road. Poor little fella 🥺

Two actual pictures of me
showing my everyday routine

"Does your dog bite?" Worse, he judges you

Me before christmas
vs me after christmas

little foot

lil foot

SOUNDCLOUD

$25
$5 shipping

$30
Free shipping

my last two brain cells after I accidentally said 'love you' to the bus driver instead of 'thank you'

hate when older people say "you're too young to be tired" alright margaret you're too old to be alive but here we are

The year is 2017. Memes are now illegal, the government has taken full control of the internet, there are no more memes available, meme guards are everywhere, meme dealers whisper memes to those who are willing to pay $150 in dark alleyways, children everywhere are crying, the world has come to an end. The world is truly.....memeingless

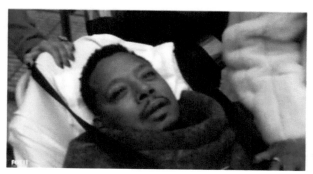

me: *bites inside of cheek when chewing on food*

me:

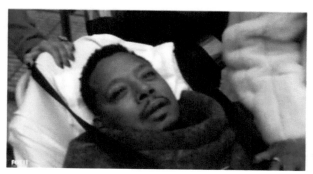

*hits blunt*

Bruh if you think about it, the brain named itself

lmao they turned cars into a real thing

Damn how hard is it to spell Brandon?
@Starbucks

Naming Link "my dude" turns everyone you meet into a very chill bro

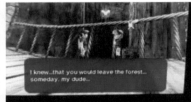

I knew...that you would leave the forest... someday, my dude...

my dude... Welcome...

"This is my dude... He is under my orders to save Hyrule."

INTERNATIONAL: Bored man hacks into giant billboard so he can play Runescape while stuck in traffic

**By Independent (UK)**
October 6, 2016

j  13    s    b    f    h    o   13 SHARES

When you and your friend were supposed
to hang out but you both knew it wasn't
going to happen

*shakes box*

I hope it's a dog

U don't know concentration until u have
to carry this from the sink to the fridge

When the groupchat is in crisis but
you kinda like the drama

# Students drank so much alcohol at college frat party that air in house registered on breathalyser, police say

When your boss comes around so you have to pretend like you're working on something

My neighbors just added Santa hats to their Halloween decorations

what if i was cool

oh wait

i am

it's almost that time.

**STAR WARS SPOILER**

cashier: your card isn't working, do
you want me to try again?
me: yes

everyone's getting into relationships and you know what im getting?

some more food brb

after eating 37 olives straight out of jar while standing in front of refrigerator at 1:34am

2:12am... going back for more olive

When your teacher asks where you see yourself in 10 years

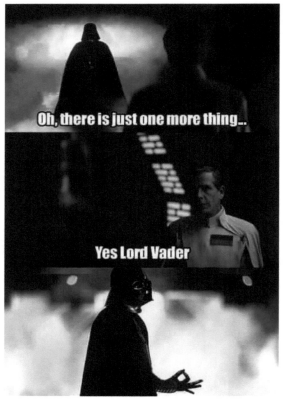

He gon be out in three days😂😂😂

when the check engine light comes on
and you don't know shit about cars but
you're an independent woman who don't
need no man

everyone else at the party

Me

OFFENSIVE JOKES

So my dad waited all year to drop this certified dad joke 🧑‍🎄 #Christmas 🍪

*bits of coin*

When you take your girl to mcdonalds for her birthday and she start lookin a little too far from the dollar menu

when u real sad tryin not to cry and then the moment someone asks "is everything ok?"

Might as well become a console since y'all tryna play me anyways

# Never travel with this guy

# I believe Japan doesn't yet understand Christmas

goes college daily, nothing happens.
when you skip one day:

# Stay in school

Sun was in my eyes lol but my new favorite picture 📷

Like   Comment   Stop Notifications   Share

👍 2 people like this.

if the sun was in ur eyes then why is ur shadow in front of u
5 mins · Like

You see your shadow when it's sunny outside dumbass...Stay in school
3 mins · Like

if the sun was in front of you your shadow would be behind you
2 mins · Like

Write a comment

I can't imagine the things this hotel air
conditioner has seen

When you asked your parents for some
legos for Christmas but they get a divorce
instead

Living with your parents vs. living on your own

Her.- do you have a dog or a cat?
me.- I don't know.

this scene is so sad. vader made a
nice meal for everyone and han
solo just starts shooting like a
dickhead

A deer entered a shop. The owner
decided to give him some biscuits. He
left...half an hour later he came back
with the squad

MESSAGES                                           now
FBI
hey, hang in there buddy

# Google

why am i always so sad and anxious    ×    Q

Weather      Sports      Entertainment      Eat & Drink

new years resolution: "Eat Healthy!
Don't do drugs! Always look your best!"

january 1st:

When your friend is about to do some stupid shit but you kind of want to see what happens

For only $6 a month, you can help this Ugandan find de way

I can hear the "wowwwww" from here

**Owen Activity** @OwenActivityy
Owen Wilson staring down a paparazzi

Stress level: the part in Chicken Run where
Babs knits her own noose

Teacher: use dandelion in a sentence

Jamaican: de cheetah is faster dandelion

Whole class:

ROCK AROUND THE CHRISTMAS TREE

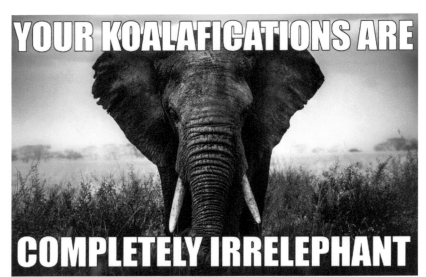

When people get mad and speed past you and y'all end up at the same red light together.

Boys with facial hair 😍

can a crip donate blood

can a teacher give a homeless kid
homework

what color are mirrors

what does water taste like

if i weigh 99 pounds and eat a pound
of nachos, am i 1% nacho

Read 22:13

if sperm makes babies and is found in
testicles then ball really is life

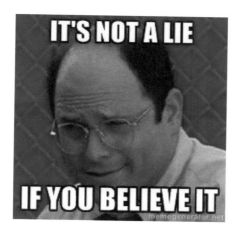

# Dwayne "The Wok" Johnson

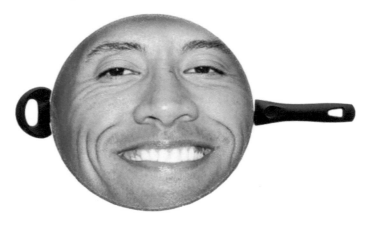

When you're sleeping and your alarm didn't ring yet but the amount of sleep you're getting is suspicious

When someone ask if you know the person who knows the way

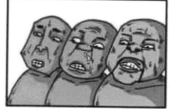

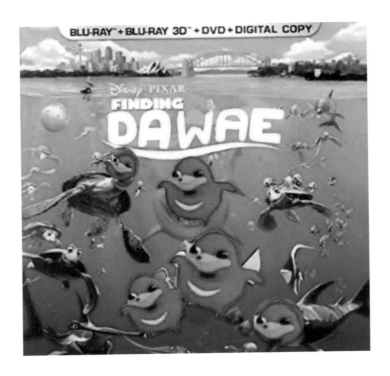

When someone says "heck" on your christian minecraft server and you let it slide but then just 10 minutes later he says "frick"

When you're taking a while to order, and hear the person behind you in line say "omg" under their breath.

When you refuse to poo on any toilet but your own and you finally make it home 💩🤍

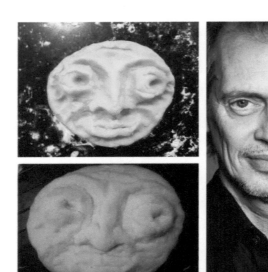

A cookie that looks like Steve Buscemi 😂😂😂

**When you're about to leave work and the boss says "Before you go.."**

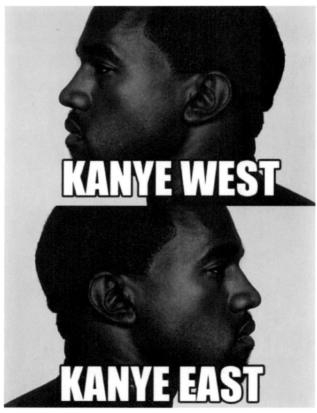

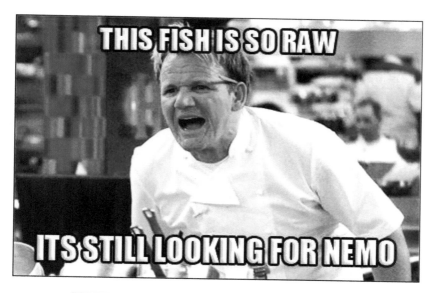

THIS FISH IS SO RAW

ITS STILL LOOKING FOR NEMO

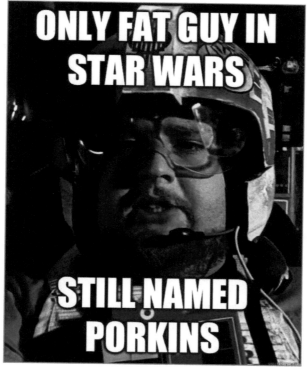

ONLY FAT GUY IN
STAR WARS

STILL NAMED
PORKINS

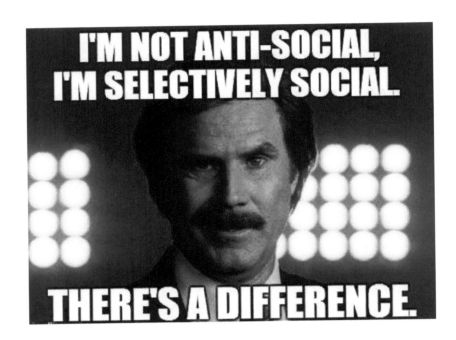

I'M NOT ANTI-SOCIAL, I'M SELECTIVELY SOCIAL. THERE'S A DIFFERENCE.

STOP MAKING ME LAUGH YOU'LL MAKE ME PUMA PANTS

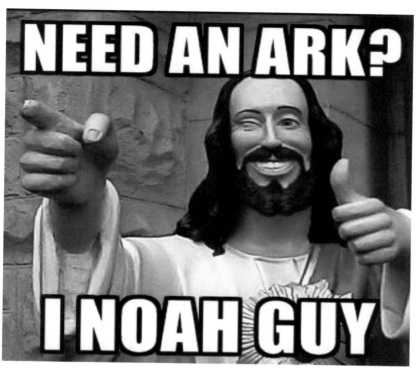

IF NICOLAS CAGE CAN STILL GET WORK

THEN YOU CAN DO ANYTHING

WHEN YOU'RE THE REASON

FOR THE COMPANY SAFETY VIDEO

When your friends are making plans
without you and you gotta act like
you don't care

Snapechat

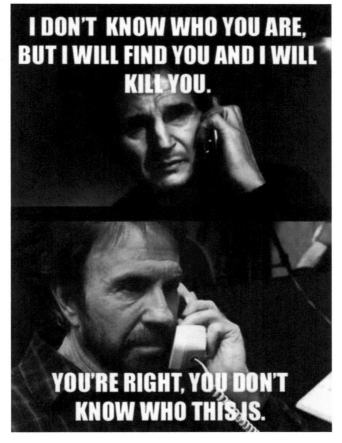

when the netflix asks if ur "still watching"
and u see ur reflection in the black screen

runs-on-ramen:

necessary

he needs those parts for his space ship

he's going to otter space

THAT AWKWARD MOMENT WHEN

YOU'VE ALREADY SAID "WHAT?" THREE TIMES N STILL HAVE NO IDEA WHAT THE PERSON SAID. SO YOU JUST AGREE

|ORANGE|
is the new BLACK|

THAT FACE YOU MAKE
WHEN YOUR MOM MAKES
YOUR FAVOURITE FOOD

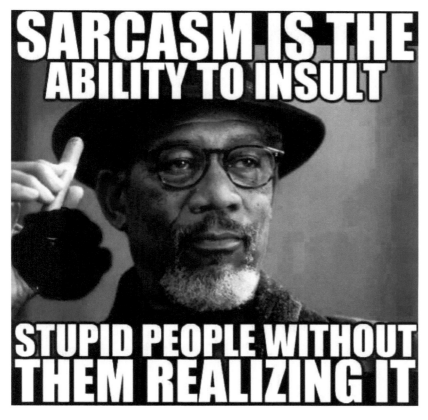

SARCASM IS THE
ABILITY TO INSULT
STUPID PEOPLE WITHOUT
THEM REALIZING IT

trying to walk when
you're drunk

When your parents make a joke
and you need money

Dwane "The Bop" Johnson

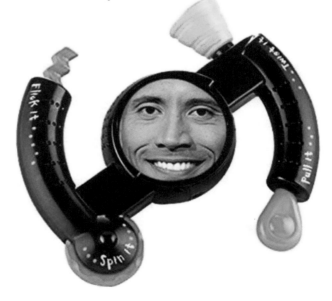

when you call shotgun but end up in the back

Dwayne "the Spock" Johnson

WHEN UR THE ONLY PERSON
WHO SAW THE
FIGHT IN SCHOOL

Whenever I'm in a group photo everyone
else looks good and I end up looking like

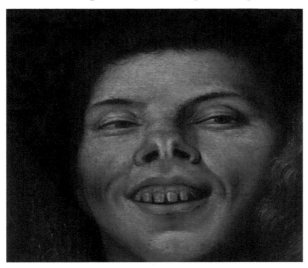

I HAVE NO IDEA

WHAT I'M DOING

2pm, a local gas station. Drake gently runs his hand across the hood of the car as he fills his tank.

"now only one of us is empty" he thinks

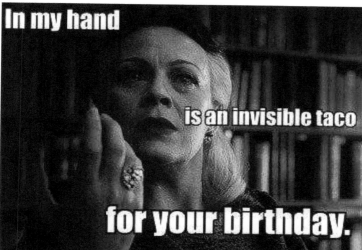

when you high in front of your parents

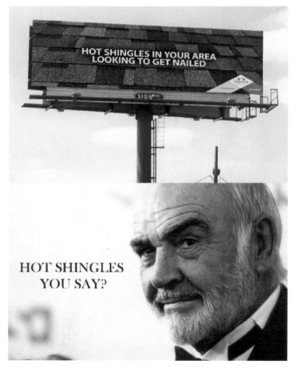

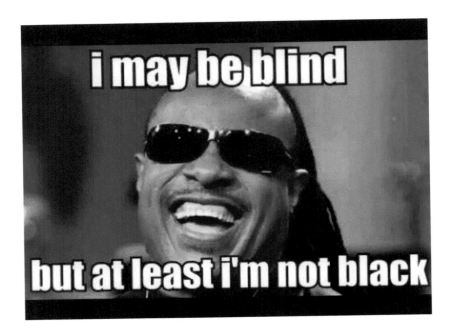

JUST HOLD ON

WE'RE GOING HOME

I DON'T ALWAYS PASS BUT WHEN I DO

I DON'T

Master has given Leo an Oscar

Leo is free

When your owner comes home
smelling like a different dog..

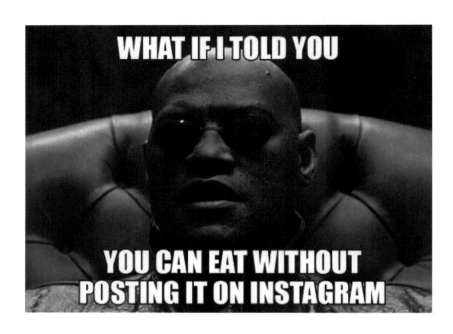

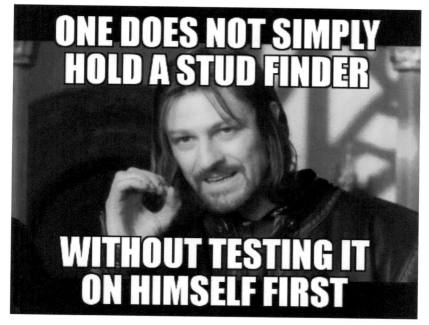

Wife rolls eyes...

THIS LAMB IS SO UNDERCOOKED

IT'S FOLLOWING MARY TO SCHOOL

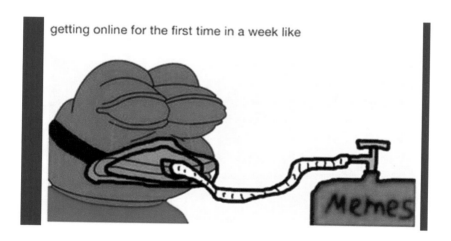

getting online for the first time in a week like

Memes

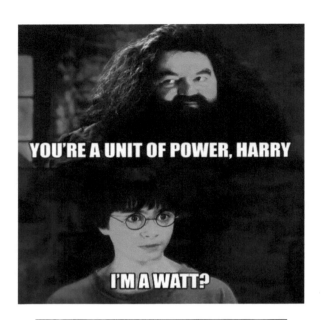

WHAT DOESN'T KILL YOU

WILL HOPEFULLY TRY AGAIN

when your mom gets home and
the atmosphere of fun and
relaxation is gone and she start
yelling for no reason

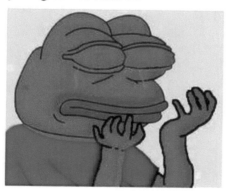

## Conclusion

Thanks again for taking the time to download this book!

You should now have a good understanding of memes , where they come from and what they are.

If you enjoyed this book, please take the time to leave me a review on Amazon. I appreciate your honest feedback, and it really helps me to continue producing high quality books.

Simply CLICK HERE to leave a review, or click on the link: (Insert link here).

CPSIA information can be obtained
at www.ICGtesting.com
Printed in the USA
BVHW022040230922
647853BV00001B/1